Classic Cars
CADILLAC

Acknowledgements.

The publishers would like to offer their special thanks to the following for their invaluable assistance in the preparation of this book:
Auburn-Cord-Duesenberg Museum, Auburn, Indiana.
Curt Marketti
Skip and Cathy Marketti
Sanderson's Auto Sales, Auburn, Ind.
Gary and Lori Shuman
The Randinelli family
Don Peterson
Charles Coleman and 'Toni'
Ben Caskey and family
Rick Carroll
The Elliott Museum, Jensen Beach, Fla.
Tom Lester
The Riekes
Hadzera Wright
All photographs taken on Asahi Pentax 6x7 with 150mm Takumar lens.
Processing by Langley Colour Labs. Langley Street, London and Unique Color Lab., Fort Wayne, Indiana. With thanks to Arthur, Tom and Roger.
Captioning supplied by Michael Sedgwick, with thanks.

Featuring the photography of Nicky Wright.
First English edition published by Colour Library Books.
© 1983 Illustrations and Text: Colour Library International Ltd.
  99 Park Avenue, New York, N.Y. 10016, U.S.A.
This edition is published by Crescent Books
Distributed by Crown Publishers, Inc.
Colour separations by Fercrom Barcelona, Spain
Display and text filmsetting by Acesetters Ltd., Richmond, Surrey, England.
Printed and bound in Barcelona, Spain by Cayfosa and Eurobinder
ISBN 0-517-405563
Crescent 1983

Dep. Leg B. 17.216/83

Cadillac is the American luxury car. It proudly proclaims itself Standard of the World. And that is no idle boast. With annual sales consistently over the 300,000 mark, Cadillac is the world's leader in the luxury car trade. And the Cadillac story is a fascinating tale told in innovative early designs, classic coachwork, legendary V12 and V16 cars and styling leadership through the decades.

Cadillac owes its name to Le Sieur Antoine de la Cadillac, the Frenchman who discovered the area now called Detroit. That's fitting because Cadillac has called Detroit, Michigan home for the past 80-plus years. Millions of Cadillacs have been built since the first, one-cylinder, 1902 model and there have been many changes in the Cadillac organization. General Motors purchased Cadillac in 1908 and founder Henry Leland left the company nine years later. Cadillac prospered through the roaring twenties and survived the Great Depression. But through the years, Cadillac was surely and steadily building a reputation as the American luxury car.

The Cadillac mystique has entered the language. We speak of the Cadillac of watches, of machinery or of whatever is deemed the best in its field. In this volume, we'll examine the Cadillac of cars.

Henry Leland operated a machine shop in the Detroit area in the 1890s, and was known throughout the community for his devotion to precision of measurement and quality work. Ransom E. Olds soon took note of Leland's fine work and contracted with him to provide engines for the new Olds car. But Olds was more interested in cost than in quality so Leland lost the contract in 1901. He returned, temporarily, to the machine tool business.

Meanwhile, the original Henry Ford Company, founded in 1899, was going through liquidation. Henry Ford would soon start another concern, the Ford Motor Company, but Leland saw an opportunity. He talked with some former Ford employees and they agreed to install Leland's engine in a jointly-designed car. The result was called Cadillac.

The first Cadillac was built in the summer of 1902 in Detroit but volume production didn't begin until early 1903. These cars were called Model A's and they were similar in appearance to the first Ford cars. They were two-seaters, featured Leland-design one-cylinder engines and the overall weight was 1,395 pounds. Top speed was about 30 mph and the advertised price was $750. The Cadillac was not yet a high-priced car but it was already earning a reputation as a carefully engineered automobile.

Cadillac found immediate success with its first car. William E. Metzger, Sales Manager for the Cadillac Automobile Company, was instrumental in building interest in the new car. Soon orders were coming in faster than the cars could be built. By the end of 1903, a total of 2,497 Cadillacs had been sold.

Cadillac's engineering was also drawing rave reviews. In 1903 a Model A was imported to England where it competed in a rugged hill climb. Although the Cadillac was pitted against many more powerful cars, it turned in a very creditable performance. Later that year, the same Model A took a first in its class in England's famous Thousand Miles Trial.

A new line of Cadillacs was introduced in 1904. Called the Model B, the new model featured four-passenger room and more luxurious accommodations. It was more massive in appearance than the Model A, which also remained in production, but retained the Leland one-cylinder engine.

There was a reorganization in 1904 and the Cadillac Automobile Company became the Cadillac Motor Car Company. Henry Leland was named General Manager, a post he was to hold until 1917.

Cadillac entered the market for luxury vehicles in 1905, an area it would come to dominate, with the Model D. A four-cylinder car, the Model D had room for five passengers in a touring car body and a wheelbase of 100 inches. It was a dramatically bigger car than the various one-cylinder Cadillacs that remained in production and its base price was over $2,800. In 1905 Cadillac would have the distinction of being the world's leading producer of automobiles. The year's total was 3,712 cars, including 156 Model D's. It would be another three years before Henry Ford would revolutionize the world of automobiles with his Model T.

Cadillac's first closed cars were built in 1906. The La Mothe Cadillac family's coat of arms also became a corporate trademark that year. The famous one-cylinder cars, facing competitive pressure from multi-cylinder car makers, were quietly being phased out. The last "one" was built in 1908.

"Standard of the World" was first used as a Cadillac advertising slogan in

Prices on the new La Salle ranged from $2,495 to $2,695; considerably less than the asking prices on the standard Cadillac line. There were eleven body styles available, including coupés, convertibles and sedans. In the whole 1927 Cadillac line, there were over 50 separate body styles available.

In its first year on the market, Cadillac sold 26,807 La Salles. In total, the division registered more than 47,000 cars in 1927, a record figure.

Models that helped Cadillac increase its market share in the boom year of 1927 included an open-front Fleetwood limousine, a number of "Imperial" models with dividers between the passenger compartments and the chauffeur's space and a wide range of handsomely styled coupés and sedans. The Earl influence in Art and Color was already reaping dividends.

Cadillac offered a total of 32 custom body designs. Several models were priced in excess of $5,000 and that was in 1927 dollars!

The 1928 Cadillacs, now called the Series 341, featured styling changes and a bored-out V8 displacing 341 cubic inches. The La Salle entered its second model year as the Series 303, again in reference to its V8 engine displacement. Bodies on all Cadillacs were lower, longer and a wider assortment of colors and interior fabric choices were available. Cadillac built over 56,000 cars, a record that would not be exceeded until 1941. La Salle production, however, sagged to 16,038 units.

Packard was still the leader in the luxury car field and there was a new competitor on the scene in 1928 . . . Duesenberg. The Duesenberg Company only built chassis; custom builders provided the body. The new auto maker was to build a rather heady reputation for itself, but Cadillac wasn't standing still either.

There were few changes as the calendar turned to 1929. For the auto industry and for the rest of the economy, it seemed certain that the wave of prosperity would last forever. But the dark days of October 1929 will remain forever etched into the memories of Americans who lived through them. That was the month the stock market crashed, rudely ending the decade known as "The Roaring Twenties."

During the halcyon days of 1929, Cadillac had been busy preparing the finest cars it would ever build. They entered a confused market with a series of supremely elegant, technological marvels. These were the

Cadillac V16 and V12, cars that would be the ultimate symbols of wealth in a time that would see little of it.

Nineteen-thirty began as a relatively quiet year for Cadillac. The standard models and the La Salle were only moderately changed from previous years. A total of 21 body styles was available in the standard Cadillac line, including seven Fisher production styles and 14 semi-customs from Fleetwood. As usual, the Fleetwood styles included open-front town cars, sedans, coupés, roadsters and convertible sedans.

The 1930 La Salle looked more "Cadillac" than before, dropping some of the Hispano-Suiza influence seen on earlier models. The La Salle continued, though, at the sporty end of the Cadillac line and was available in phaeton, roadster and convertible versions in addition to the standard sedans and coupés.

But the most fabulous Cadillac of them all was waiting in the wings. Announced in December 1929, the V16 was stunning news for the automotive world in general and for Cadillac's competitors in particular.

The Cadillac V16 was a beautiful design and an engineering tour de force. The creation of Cadillac engineer Owen Nacker, the 452 cubic inch V16 was more than an engine, it was a statement by Cadillac; a declaration that the finest cars in the world were now being made in a General Motors plant in Detroit, Michigan. That was a point open to contention but nobody could deny that the 1930 Series 452 V16's were the grandest Cadillacs ever built.

The V16 was offered in a choice of 54 Fleetwood body styles and prices ranged from $5,700 to over $9,000. Models of note included the famous Madam X sedans with leaning windshields, superb coachwork and distinctive styling touches. Other V16 models included a dual-cowl phaeton, convertible sedans and a dashing roadster. Yet the majority of Cadillac V16's, to the chagrin of collectors today, were made in standard sedan form.

The timing couldn't have been worse for Cadillac's new prestige leader. The depression was just getting underway and consumer confidence was rapidly disappearing. At first it seemed that the very rich wouldn't be affected by the business downturn. A total of 2,887 V16's were sold in 1930. But the next year's sales reports would bring bad tidings for the maker of the V16 and a new companion model.

Henry Martyn Leland, the "Master of Precision," known as the father of the Cadillac, died in 1930 at the age of 90. It was just 30 years earlier that the first one-cylinder Cadillac had been built.

Cadillac dropped the other shoe in 1931. It announced the availability of a new 368 cubic inch V12 line of cars. Cadillac was now in the unique position of offering four distinct lines of cars: the V8 La Salle, the standard Cadillac V8, the mighty V16, and the new V12.

The new V12, named the Series 370, was a step above the regular Cadillac and just below the V16 in price. However, the V12 cut deeply into sales of the V16, of which only 364 were sold in '31. In the depressed economy, there obviously were many luxury car buyers who considered the V12 better value than the 16.

The standard 1931 Cadillacs and La Salles, at the peak of the classic period in American car styling, were very impressive automobiles. Distinctive new styling touches included the substitution of ventilation doors for the traditional louvers on the hood sides and a chrome-plated screen over the radiator. The styling of this car was especially pleasing and would be copied by other manufacturers, notably Chevrolet, in the years ahead.

In 1931 there was new competition for the Cadillac V16, notably the Marmon 16, but this had little effect on sales since few people could afford either one. In any body style, the 1931 Cadillacs were magnificent examples of the finest era of custom coachwork in automotive history.

Nineteen thirty two was the last year for classic styling in the Cadillac line. After this year, there would be no more tombstone-type radiators and clamshell fenders. The Cadillac line remained mechanically unchanged in all engine types but there was new competition in the supercar fringe area. Lincoln, Packard and Pierce-Arrow all made V12's available. But as the Depression grew worse, nobody was selling many of them. Total Cadillac sales slid to 8,084, its worst figures since 1918.

All the 1933 Cadillacs and La Salles showed dramatic styling changes. Streamlining was taking hold of automotive design and body lines were becoming more integrated. It is here, in the 1933 Cadillacs, that we see the beginnings of the modern automobile. Prices now ranged from under $2,800 for a La Salle roadster to over $6,000 for a custom-bodied Fleetwood V16. Cadillac was well aware of the diminishing market for its V16 super cars but it was desperate to maintain some semblance of volume production. The division placed advertisements in Fortune and other prestigious publications. In these ads, prospective customers were urged to order their V16's early because they were being reserved for Society's "400." The ads were wildly optimistic. Cadillac managed to retail only 126 V16's in 1933, as the ravages of the Depression continued. In all four lines, Cadillac was only able to sell 6,655 cars.

Of interest to many collectors today are the "Gothic-design" and "cathedral-like" hearses of the early thirties. Packard continued to sell many commercial chassis but Cadillac was becoming a leader in the lucrative prestige car market. All commercial applications were on the Cadillac V8 chassis.

As the end of the 1933 selling season approached, it was evident that the La Salle line was in trouble. It just wasn't achieving the kind of volume Cadillac had envisioned for a medium-price entry and there was continued pressure from financial advisers to drop the line altogether. But Harley Earl's proposal for 1934 gave the La Salle a reprieve.

The 1934 La Salle was a truly modern car and it was re-positioned to be more of a volume seller. Gone was the V8, replaced by a straight eight engineered by Oldsmobile. Other new mechanical features included knee-action independent front suspension.

But it was the styling that was drawing the rave reviews. New for '34 was a narrow, vertical grille design that would remain a La Salle trademark for years.

The other models in the 1934 line were restyled and the beginning of an economic recovery was in the making. Cadillac retailed 13,014 cars in the model year, including 7,195 La Salles, but only 60 V16's.

Cadillac introduced new series designations in 1935. The standard Cadillac V8's were now available as Series 10, Series 20 and Series 30. The V12 was now labelled the Series 40 and the V16, pride of the line, became the Series 60. Even though it was on the bottom rung of the Cadillac ladder, the La Salle was now referred to as the Series 50.

The all-steel "turret-top" was introduced on 1935 model closed cars. Styling was along lines similar to the 1933-34 cars.

The introduction of the medium-price Packard 120 was of great concern to Cadillac in 1935. It was Packard's first intrusion into the market for lower-priced automobiles and it was markedly more successful than the Cadillac La Salle. The sales success of the Packard 120 is credited by many with hastening the death of the La Salle.

Confusing Cadillac historians may have been the game plan but new series identification was introduced again in 1936. The La Salle was, as before, the Series 50. Next in the pricing structure was the Series 60 Cadillac V8. The 60 was another competitor for the Packard 120. Cadillac introduced a new V8 in '36 and the 60 was powered by a smaller 333 cubic inch version of it. The Series 70 and Series 75 were V8's, of 346 cubic inch displacement. The V12's continued as the Series 80 and 85 and the V16 Cadillac was now called the Series 90.

The La Salle had adopted hydraulic brakes in 1934 and now it was the standard Cadillac's turn. The industry was recovering from the setbacks of the Depression and Cadillac enjoyed its best sales year since 1929. A total of 25,884 Cadillacs were sold, including just 52 V16's. Of these V16's, three were bare chassis shipped to outside coachbuilders.

Nineteen thirty-seven was a year of considerable styling changes for the Cadillac and the La Salle model line in particular. Not only did the La Salle have a sharp new style but, for the first time since 1933, it was powered by a Cadillac V8. The 333 cube V8, used the previous year in the Cadillac 60, was now used exclusively in the La Salle. The hot new La Salle reached a record 32,005 buyers. It was still, however, trailing behind Packard's hot-selling, junior-edition 120. Overall, Cadillac sales jumped to 46,152. It seemed that the Depression's end was finally in sight. Then Cadillac did the unexpected.

The slow-selling V16 was not dropped in 1938. Instead, a new design for the 16 was introduced. Although sales levels certainly didn't warrant it, the 1938 Cadillac V16 was an entirely new 431 cubic inch motor. This new engine was not the styling masterpiece of the earlier V16 but it was an impressive performer. It made the heavy Series 90 Cadillac a surprisingly lively piece of machinery.

The Series 90, along with the rest of the Cadillac line, was extensively restyled in 1938 with a strong horizontal bar grille and massive body lines. The V16 would remain in production through 1939 and 1940 even though production levels were disappointing. Only 315 were sold in '38, 138 in 1939 and a mere 61 in 1940. By 1940 the rest of the Cadillac line had achieved a more modern appearance than the facelifted Series 90 cars. When production finished at the end of the 1940 model year, a glorious era of custom-bodied, prestigious automobiles had come to a close. There never would be another car like the Cadillac V16.

With the introduction of the Sixty Special sedan in 1938, it was clear that Cadillac was America's style leader. The car was young stylist Bill Mitchell's design. He would later become chief stylist for the General Motors Corporation. The Sixty Special was an especially influential automobile because it didn't have any running boards and it imparted a new "Cadillac sedan" look that would influence American car design for years to come. In fact, the 1971-76 Cadillac Fleetwood Brougham sedans, with their handsome side window treatment, are an interesting throwback to the lines of the 1938 Sixty Special.

Sales declined in 1938 as the American economy took a brief turn for the worse. The '39 Cadillacs had a new look with a Buick-like two-tiered grille. As the tumultuous decade drew to a close, there was hope that the Forties would bring the long delayed economic recovery.

It would be a recovery but it would be brought on by war.

The 1940 model year marked the end of one era and the beginning of another. The day of the classic car, marked by extravagance and low production, was now at an end. Nineteen-forty was the last year for the venerable V16 and also the final model year for the companion Cadillac, La Salle. It was also the end of the line for the custom body builder.

In its place came an efficient line of Cadillac cars, including a moderately facelifted Sixty Special sedan and a handsome line of convertibles, sedans and coupés. The four-door convertible remained a highly regarded prestige item in the Cadillac line-up.

In its final season, La Salle retained its traditionally slim vertical grille design and its small version of the Cadillac V8. There were two series within the La Salle range this year. One was a carryover Series 50 and the other was a brand new Series 52 featuring GM's bold torpedo-style body design. Many collectors consider the 1940 Series 52 La Salle to be one of the nicest. It has aged gracefully.

Only 61 V16 Cadillacs were built in the 1940 model year. And these, compared to the standard Cadillac line, had a somewhat dated look about them. The day of the complex, ostentatious V16 luxury car had clearly come to an end. The V16 was discontinued at the end of the 1940 model year but its accomplishment was great indeed. The V16 had placed Cadillac at the forefront of American luxury car production. From the day it was born, the Cadillac V16 was regarded as something sensational and, through the years, a great percentage of these cars have been saved for appreciating collectors.

Something of a watershed year, 1940 was also the last season for the sidemounted spare tire and the first for sealed beam headlamps. Running boards were now an option and in a year they would be gone from all models, save the Series 75 limousine.

Cadillac was hitting its stride in 1941. Bold new styling featured a grille design that would come to mean only "Cadillac" in the coming years. The '41 Cadillac set a styling trend for American cars, with its massive design, for years to come. But in 1941 there was nothing like it on the American roads.

The La Salle and the V16 were discontinued but in their place was an important innovation Oldsmobile had pioneered the previous year. Called Hydra Matic, it was the world's first fully automatic transmission. With its successful '41 cars, Cadillac set a sales record for the model year . . . 66,130 cars. But war clouds were on the horizon.

Nineteen forty-two was Cadillac's 40th year of car production and there was brand new styling to commemorate the event. The Sixty Special received its first new body since Bill Mitchell's classic 1938 design but it shed some of its exclusivity in the process. Cadillac's bold eggcrate grille was even more prominent. New offerings included fastback coupés, available in Series 61 and Series 62 form. The fastback look would spread to many other makes before the forties were through. The Series 75 limousines retained their conservative 1941 styling but did receive the new '42 grille work. Hydra Matic was proving very popular in its second year. Over 60 per cent of the 1942 cars were equipped with it.

But 1942 was destined to be a short model year for American auto manufacturers. On December 7, 1941, the Japanese bombed Pearl Harbor and the United States became involved in World War II. The last '42 Cadillac was built on February 4, 1942. The final 2,150 cars featured black-out trim instead of chrome, as auto makers tried to conserve materials vital to the war effort.

For three long years, no Cadillac automobiles were produced. Cadillac turned out tanks in its Detroit plants for the duration of the war.

When peace finally returned, plenty of demand for new cars had built up. Cadillac turned out 1946 models, basically updated '42's, to a car-hungry public but demand far outran supply. The 1946 V8 was called the "Battle-Proved" engine and it did boast of a number of improvements gained from experience during World War II tank use. Cadillac built only 29,142 cars during the shortened 1946 model year.

The 1947 model year was a rerun of 1946. The Cadillac design, dating to 1942, was aging but the supply of new Cadillacs still had not caught up with demand. Cadillac sold over 60,000 cars in 1947 and had unfilled orders for almost 100,000 more. There would be a brand new Cadillac in 1948.

The 1950s were really the golden age for Cadillac. And the fifties were previewed in 1948 and 1949 with a dramatic one-two punch that would set the competition reeling. With the styling of the '48's and the engineering advances of the '49's, Cadillac set a pattern of leadership that took up where the V16 had left off.

The new postwar 1948 Cadillac was a beautiful, if somewhat unconventional, design. Beautiful were the flowing lines and the boldly Cadillac frontal styling. Shocking was the way the rear fenders culminated in brashly upswept "tail fins." The fins were the inspiration of Harley Earl who reportedly got the idea after examining a new Lockheed P-38 fighter plane. Soon his drawings were all showing the tail fins. Cadillac dealers, known for their conservative tastes, were nervous. But there was no need to worry. Cadillac sales shot up higher than the fins.

Over 90 per cent of the 52,000 Cadillacs sold in 1948 were equipped with the optional Hydra Matic. It wouldn't, however, replace the three-speed manual as standard equipment until 1953.

The three-speed manual was not the only holdover from an earlier age. The prestigious Cadillac 75 limo was still dressed in its 1941 suit of clothes. A new Cadillac limousine would not appear until 1950.

The dramatic new styling had appeared in '48 but the engine that went with it was delayed until 1949. This new V8, a 331 cubic inch design, was a real trend setter. An overhead valve V8, it was much more compact than the old motor but put out a solid 160 hp. Together with its running mate, the 1949 Oldsmobile Rocket V8, it was the engine of the future. The fifties would see the rush to the overhead valve V8 and they would remain the dominant American engine well into the eighties.

Cadillac was still holding one card up its sleeve, though. That was the 1949 Coupé de Ville, introduced in mid-season. The Coupé de Ville, along with the companion Buick Riviera and Oldsmobile Holiday, were the first true production hardtops. The Coupé de Ville was an immediate success and it would, one day, become the most popular Cadillac of them all.

Cadillac styling got bulkier in 1950 but retained the successful themes introduced in 1948-49. The Cadillac grille remained dominant as did the now familiar tail fins. Cadillac was developing, along with Oldsmobile, a reputation as the fast American car. Two Cadillacs were even entered in the prestigious Le Mans road race in France and they *placed!*

New for 1952 was the Cadillac 75 limousine. It finally shed its prewar look in favor of a contemporary style fully compatible with the rest of the Cadillac line. Cadillac sales shot over the 100,000 mark for the first time in history.

Nineteen fifty-one was a year of minor changes throughout the Cadillac line. The Series 61, a low volume price leader, was dropped in mid-year. Cadillac sold 110,340 cars in 1951.

Again in 1952, there were few changes. Cadillac prices now ranged from $3,542 for the 62 two-door hardtop to $5,572 for the 75 limousine. The glamor queen of the Cadillac range was the flashy 62 convertible, of which only 6,400 were built.

Although styling changes were kept to a minimum again in 1953, the car was unmistakeably "The Standard of the World" and the luxury leader on the American highway. Cadillac was fast, opulent and radiated success from every angle. The tail fins remained the focal point of the rear fender line and the massive grille was all-Cadillac.

New for 1953 was a super-luxurious limited production convertible that brought added status to the entire Cadillac line. Called the Eldorado, the new car was one of three special convertibles that GM introduced in mid-1953. The others were the Oldsmobile Fiesta and the Buick Sky Lark. General Motors promoted them as "dream cars" available to the public. The 1953 Eldorado was listed at a stratospheric $7,750, much higher than even the 75 limousine. The 62 convertible, for example, was listed at only $4,143. Eldorado exclusives included a wraparound windshield, cut down doors, wire wheels and a lavish interior

The Eldorado convertible received prominent attention when it was used as President Eisenhower's official inauguration parade car in January 1953. With its imposing price tag, it remained a very exclusive piece of machinery. Only 532 were built.

The 1954 Cadillacs were completely restyled, with wraparound windshields on all models, a wider grille and especially sleek styling on the popular Series 62 hardtops and Coupé de Villes.

The Sixty Special was still the fanciest four-door sedan available but the rich and famous continued to view the 75 limousine with particular favor. The Eldorado convertible was now a fancy version of the 62 and its price tag was "just" $5,738 that year. But a Series 62 ragtop could be had for $4,404. In any event, in 1954, there was no better status symbol than a red Cadillac convertible.

The auto industry enjoyed a record year in 1955 and so did Cadillac. Changes were in detail only, but sales rocketed to 140,777. The Eldorado did receive new rear sheet metal with sharp new fins. The Eldorado look would appear on other Cadillac models, but not until 1958!

Horsepower ratings went up in '55, although displacement remained at 331 cubic inches; advertised horsepower was now 250.

The 1956 Cadillacs were practically indistinguishable from the '55's. The traditional eggcrate grille was replaced with a fine textured design. A four-door hardtop was a new addition and it became Cadillac's sales leader in its very first year. A companion for the Eldorado convertible was announced;

the Eldorado Seville hardtop. With that, the convertible became known as the Eldorado Biarritz. Horsepower rating on these special models was boosted to 305.

The 1957 Cadillac was all new, from road to roof. The chassis featured a new X-type frame and the body was longer, lower and wider in the best fifties tradition. The wraparound windshield now had reverse-sloping A pillars and the tail fin design and height was as impressive as ever.

But the biggest news was the introduction of a new Cadillac rivalling the V16 of two decades earlier for sheer luxury. Called the Eldorado Brougham, the new car was introduced in response to the limited production Lincoln Continental of 1956-57. The Continental had not been much of a success, especially with its $10,000 price tag but the Eldorado topped that . . . with a suggested list price of $13,074. For his money, the buyer received four-door luxury, air suspension, exclusive sheet metal and an almost unbelievable host of electrical gadgets. Cadillac General Manager James M. Roche asserted that this was "the finest car possible." Exactly 400 were produced in the 1957 model year.

The Cadillac V8 was rated at 300 horsepower on the standard 1957 models and 325 on the Eldorado Brougham. The Eldorado Biarritz and Seville could be had with the 325 hp version at extra cost. Its distinguishing feature was two four-barrel carburetors. In the recession year of 1957, Cadillac sales dropped slightly to 146,841 units.

The 1958 Cadillac was extensively restyled, although the basic structure was unchanged. Dual headlamps became standard and this year's Cadillac was very chromy, especially the Sixty Special Sedan. There were few changes to the ultra-expensive Eldorado Brougham. Production slipped to 304 units.

If the standard Cadillac wasn't long enough, an "extended deck sedan" was new for '58. It quickly became the second best selling car in the line. It, however, wasn't scheduled to return in 1959. There was no need for an extended deck version of the 1959 Cadillac.

The 1959 Cadillac was one of the most incredibly flamboyant automobiles to ever make it into actual production. This was the year the famous Cadillac tail fin reached its peak and what a peak it was. They were, literally, rocket-type fins on which bullet-like tail light bulbs were mounted. It was a particularly challenging year for the nation's funeral car makers in their annual quest to come up with dignified coaches.

In addition to the memorable tail fins, the 1959 Cadillacs featured extreme wraparound windshields, and radical upper body styling on coupés and hardtops. For the first time in several years, the Eldorado convertible and hardtop shared sheet metal with other, more pedestrian, Cadillacs. But the Eldorado Brougham was another story. The '59 Brougham was hand-built in the Turin body shop of Pininfarina. Price remained at $13,074 but sales declined to just 99 units. Styling of the Eldorado Brougham was in much better taste than that of the standard Cadillac. It was very subdued and was, in fact, a preview of the styling that would be seen on the standard 1961 Cadillac.

Cadillac's price leader in 1959 was, as in years past, the Series 62 coupé. It was now $4,892. The popular six-window sedan was priced at $5,498 in De Ville trim and the 62 convertible was now $5,455. The Sixty Special sedan was $6,233, the Eldorado convertible was listed at $7,401 and the 75 limousine was a steep $9,748.

The 1959 Cadillac was a big car and the engineers decided that a little more power was called for. The Cadillac V8 was bored out to 390 cubic inches and the hp rating was now 325. In souped-up Eldorado form, Cadillac claimed 345 horsepower.

Although still based on the 1959 body shell, Cadillac styling became more sober in 1960. The grille was cleaned up a bit and the fins were trimmed more than a little. The Eldorado Brougham made its last appearance, again with a $13,074 price attached. Only 100 were built. Interestingly, styling for that year's Eldorado set the pattern for the standard 1962 Cadillac. Model year production for the 1960 Cadillacs totaled 142,184, just 60 off the 1959 figure.

Cadillac wore brand new styling for 1961. Compact cars were making inroads into the American marketplace and a slightly trimmer Cadillac was a reflection of this trend. The Series 62 was for bargain shoppers, the De Villes were the volume leaders and the Fleetwoods were the prestigious Cadillacs. The Eldorado Biarritz convertible was the sexy one. Unfortunately, this year's Biarritz was practically indistinguishable from the popular 62 ragtop.

Even with a slightly smaller look about it, the 1961 models were all Cadillac. The fins remained an aggressive identifyer and they were joined by a pair of lower level fins along the bottom of the rear fenders. The unusual wraparound windshield of the 1959-60 cars was replaced on all but the Fleetwood 75 limousine. That model, in a move that made it appear strangely dated, retained the upper structure of the '59-'60's.

Cadillac also tested the waters for a smaller car in '61 but the move was not well received. Called the Series 62 Short Deck sedan, the car was seven inches shorter than a standard Cadillac. Only 3,756 were sold. This shorter Cadillac was also available in 1962 but was discontinued part way through the 1963 model year. It would be years before Cadillac buyers would find a compact car appealing.

Nineteen sixty-two was a year of refinement for Cadillac. The option book included cornering lights for the first time and all Cadillacs were equipped with dual master-cylinder brake systems. Production on the pleasantly-styled 1962 models reached a record 160,840.

Highlighting the 1963 Cadillacs was their conservative new styling, including a grille that was remarkably similar to the '59's. But under the hood was a new V8, with an improved power-to-weight ratio. Cubic inch displacement remained at 390.

The 1964 Cadillac still had fins but they were lower than ever. The V8 engine, already an able performer, was bored out to 429 cubic inches. The lowline 62 series retained Hydra Matic as standard equipment but a brand new three-speed torque converter Turbo Hydra Matic was now fitted as standard on De Villes and Fleetwoods. It would be standard across the line in 1965.

The 75 limousines retained their curious 1959-style upper body structure but their lower styling was compatible with the rest of the line. Production of 1964 Cadillacs set another record.

Cadillac design was brand new for 1965. Whether or not it still had fins was a matter of opinion, but there was no doubt that this was a startlingly new, very clean Caddy. A new perimeter frame replaced the cruciform-type used since 1957. Side glass was curved and frameless windows added to the airy look. The 62 Series was renamed Calais but the De Villes still accounted for the vast majority of Cadillac sales.

The distinctive Sixty Special was also restyled and was available with an optional vinyl-covered roof. Cadillac engineers and stylists had obviously worked hard on the 1965 program and, as it turned out, there wasn't enough time to bring out a new 75 limousine for the 1965 model year. The '64 was carried over until a new limo, again compatible with the rest of the line, could be introduced in 1966.

There were few changes for '66. The Fleetwood Brougham sedan became a companion model for the Sixty Special, the only difference being that the Brougham had a vinyl roof covering. This was the last year for the rear wheel drive Eldorado convertible, as there would be a brand new Eldorado coupé to replace it in 1967.

The 1967 Eldorado coupé was Cadillac's new prestige leader. The new Eldorado was a front wheel drive coupé and shared mechanics with the 1966 Olds Tornado. The Eldorado sold exceptionally well in its first year and, coupled with a restyled standard line, it helped Cadillac sell more than 200,000 cars in a single year for the first time in its history.

Styling remained intact for 1968 but a huge new 472 cubic inch V8 engine was introduced. This was, by no means, a performance engine but was designed with the proliferation of power accessories and emission controls in mind. Rated at 375 horsepower, it was the largest engine available in a 1968-model production automobile.

The American auto industry was preoccupied with meeting U.S. government safety regulations in the late sixties and the 1968 Cadillac reflected this. Standard equipment included seat belts for all passenger positions, shoulder belts for front seat occupants (except the De Ville convertible), side marker lights, padded instrument panel, energy absorbing steering column and a host of other equipment. The vast majority of Cadillacs were also being equipped with air conditioning, power steering, as well as power assisted brakes, windows and seats together with other devices to aid driver comfort.

Fresh styling greeted Cadillac buyers in 1969. All models except the Eldorado were of a decidedly modern appearance. The front vent windows, introduced in the thirties, were replaced by an improved flow-through ventilation system and almost all Cadillacs were now equipped with air conditioning.

The 1970 Cadillacs received only slight cosmetic changes but the Eldorado's engine was bored out to an incredible 500 cubic inches. The rest of the line had to be content with only 472 cubic inches of motivating force. The Eldorado engine had an advertised horsepower rating of 400. 1970 was also the last year for the De Ville convertible, a Cadillac tradition for many years, as sales of convertible models had been declining since 1965.

Nineteen seventy-one was a year of many surprises for Cadillac watchers. It was the first time the whole line had been restyled and re-engineered since 1961. All models featured dramatic new styling with severely curved side glass, very thin windshield pillars and a "classic car" grille.

The Eldorado coupé returned with controversial new styling that seemed somewhat bloated in comparison with the 1967-70 models, but the front-drive car got a new companion, an Eldorado convertible, the first since 1966. The styling of the new Eldorado ragtop reminded many of the first Eldorado model of 1953. It had the same rear fender louvers, compound curve windshield and generally imposing appearance.

The 1971 Eldorado Coupé even had "opera windows" a fad that would spread through the industry in the ensuing years. Another model that harked back to earlier days was the 1971 Sixty Special Fleetwood Brougham sedan. It featured a window design treatment remarkably similar to the first Sixty Special that had appeared in 1938. They were both Bill Mitchell creations. Mechanically, all 1971 Cadillacs featured lower compression ratios that allowed the use of regular or unleaded grade gasolines.

After the across-the-board changes in 1971, there were few styling modifications for '72. All models featured reinforced bumpers with rub strips that could "take a bump" better than earlier ones, and there was an improved ventilation system and modified emission controls. As usual, color and interior trims got their annual updates. Cadillac sales were at a record level again in 1972. In an unusual bit of global diplomacy, United States President Richard M. Nixon presented car buff Leonid Brezhnev, chairman of the U.S.S.R., with a new car, a black 1972 Cadillac Eldorado coupé.

The 1973 Eldorados featured simpler styling that eliminated the rear fender louvers and beveled rear deck of the 1971-72 cars. Radial tires were now a factory option. The standard '73 line was relatively unchanged, although front and rear bumpers were strengthened. Sales went over the 300,000 mark for the first time.

The good times came to an abrupt end in October 1973, however, when the Arabs shut off the oil. Now OPEC was calling the shots and large cars suddenly became unwanted. All this coincided with the introduction of the relatively unchanged 1974 Cadillacs. Sales fell dramatically, but by the spring of '74, people were buying Cadillacs again.

The 1975 model year began quietly for Cadillac. All models featured rectangular headlamps and the Eldorado had some new sheet metal. All Cadillacs now used the 500 cubic inch V8 engine and electronic fuel injection became an option in mid-year.

In April of that year Cadillac introduced the exciting Seville sedan. Priced at over $13,000, this was the most expensive model in the line. It was also the first small Cadillac. The Seville used a 350 cubic inch Oldsmobile V8 with fuel injection. The boxy sedan styling was an immediate sensation and was to become the pattern for the 1977 full-size cars. The first 2,000 Sevilles off the line were all painted silver with a silver interior and vinyl top.

Nineteen seventy-five will be remembered as the year Cadillac brought out a small car, while nineteen seventy-six was the year Cadillac built its last convertible. The rest of the industry had already dropped out of the ragtop business, so the 1976 Eldorado was the lost convertible made by an American manufacturer until Chrysler started making them again in 1982.

The 1976 Eldorado convertible quickly became a collector's item, with a production run of 14,000 cars. The last 200 cars off the line were all painted white with red and blue trim, in honor of America's Bi-centennial celebration.

The standard 1977 Cadillac line went through the downsizing process in fine style, with excess weight eliminated but the essence of Cadillac maintained. Sales reached record levels as buyers approved of the trimmer lines.

Only the Eldorado coupé retained its outsized 1971 vintage dimensions. All Cadillacs, save the Seville, were powered by a 425 cubic inch version of the familiar V8. The Seville was freshened up for the new year with a new grille and a "delete vinyl roof" option.

Nineteen seventy-eight was the last year for the big Eldorado. A special Biarritz coupé was offered for the occasion. It featured a special padded roof and an elaborate leather interior. Other models were unchanged.

Cadillac sales went over the 380,000 mark in 1979, a peak that remains unsurpassed. The new Eldorado coupé looked a lot like the first one, a '67 model. Cadillac customers liked what they saw and ordered more than 60,000 of them. New options included the availability of Oldsmobile diesel power. In April 1979, however, the deteriorating political situation in the Middle East forced oil prices up once again. This time the shift away from large cars appeared to be more permanent. Cadillac's 1980 model year got off to a shaky start.

The 1980 Seville, with its bustle-back trunk, was the most controversially styled car of the year and the most talked about Caddy since the '59's. From a technical standpoint, the new Seville was a knockout. It had four-wheel independent suspension, front-wheel drive, the choice of diesel or gas V8 power and disc brakes all around. It was, in fact, an Eldorado under the skin. But the skin was really something else. You either loved it or you hated it. The standard Cadillac line was reworked somewhat, with more aerodynamic sheet metal and the addition of a Fleetwood Brougham coupé to the line. Sales were down from the record 1979 levels.

In search of better fuel economy, Cadillac engineers came up with a novel concept in 1981. Called the V-8-6-4, the new 368 cubic inch engine was able to run on 8, 6, or 4 cylinders, depending on power requirements.

Cadillac buyers complained of mechanical malfunctions and the system was all but abandoned in 1982. Only 1982 and '83 Series 75 limousines were equipped with the unusual engine.

In mid-1981, Cadillac brought out a really small car, the Cimarron. The Cimarron was a General Motors J-car with Cadillac appointments and trim. It was powered by a 1.8 litre four cylinder engine and had a standard four-speed transmission. To put it mildly, this was quite a departure for Cadillac.

The full-size 1982 Cadillacs featured an aluminium 250 cubic inch V8 as standard equipment. Also available was a gas V6, supplied by Buick, and a diesel V8 engine from Oldsmobile. The Seville and Eldorado models were largely unchanged.

For '83, Cadillac gave the Cimarron a power boost via a five-speed manual transaxle and 2.0 litre four-banger. The traditionally-styled full size cars, Eldorados and Sevilles retained their previous styling.

Cadillacs have come a long way since 1902. From one-cylinder to four to eight to 12 and 16 and now, back to four again.

The specifications have changed through the years but the dedication to quality has not. It was a hard road to the top of the market in the luxury car business but Cadillac made it. Cadillac is often criticized and other cars are sometimes compared favorably to "The Standard of the World." But, as Henry Leland would have been quick to point out, that's the penalty of leadership.

Of the great American names that have survived from pioneer days – Buick, Ford, Olds and Rambler as well as Cadillac – all began with a slow-turning horizontal underfloor motor and two-speed planetary transmission. In the case of this 1903 Model-A runabout, there is but one cylinder of 98.2 ci displacement, and its respectable 9¾ horsepower gave it a top speed of 30 mph. Extras available included a $30 buggy top and $100 worth of demountable rear tonneau for two further passengers.

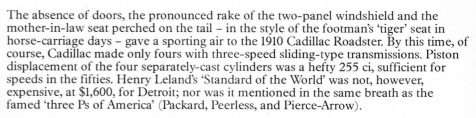

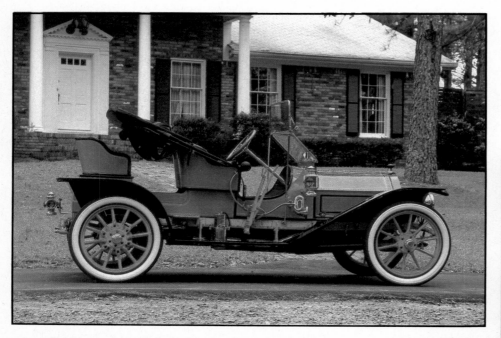

The absence of doors, the pronounced rake of the two-panel windshield and the mother-in-law seat perched on the tail – in the style of the footman's 'tiger' seat in horse-carriage days – gave a sporting air to the 1910 Cadillac Roadster. By this time, of course, Cadillac made only fours with three-speed sliding-type transmissions. Piston displacement of the four separately-cast cylinders was a hefty 255 ci, sufficient for speeds in the fifties. Henry Leland's 'Standard of the World' was not, however, expensive, at $1,600, for Detroit; nor was it mentioned in the same breath as the famed 'three Ps of America' (Packard, Peerless, and Pierce-Arrow).

The two ends of Cadillac Division's product-spectrum in 1931 were represented by the LaSalle 345A five-passenger coupé *top left and bottom right,* a modest V-8 costing $2,295, and the Model-452A Cadillac Sixteen *below and facing page* on which town car prices ran in the $7,000-9,000 bracket. This actual example has been converted from a sedan. Even the true Plain Jane of the Cadillac family, the 1929 LaSalle 328 five-passenger sedan *bottom left* had style, its radiator suggestive of a Hispano-Suiza's. The sidelamps had just been moved from cowl to front fenders. Fixed wood wheels and demountable rims were standard equipment on 1929 Cadillacs and LaSalles.

With its streamline cowl, electric lights, and left-hand steering – all found on 1914 Cadillacs – the underhood revolution on this 1915 Model-51 touring car isn't immediately apparent. One might be looking at a late example of the familiar Thirty. Not so: 1915 was the first year of the 90-degree V-8 L-head motor, a layout destined to dominate Cadillac thinking for over thirty years. What started, however, with 314 ci and 70 horsepower ended up with over double the output, from a piston displacement less than ten per cent greater.

Pre-Classic era Cadillac: the 1924 V-63 five-passenger coupé with body by Fisher. Beneath the surface lies the smoothness of the new 90-degree crankshaft and the stopping power of the *marque's* first four-wheel brakes. Closed-car refinements include a ventilating windshield, a big sun vizor, and even some limited trunk space on this body style – sedans and tourings made do with a trunk rack. A second spare tire and rim came extra, and a few more years would elapse before front bumpers became regular equipment, even if this coupé wore quarter-bumpers at the back. The dashboard *below left* is plain, if well stocked, with drum speedometer and odometer, while the motor *below right* is likewise innocent of the high finish so often found on European contemporaries.

The ultimate in V-16s? A 1930 Model-452 Fleetwood two-passenger convertible coupé with the Madam-X type slightly slanted vee-windshield, and the sweep-panel two-toning pioneered by LeBaron's Ralph Roberts. All the 'Classic' equipment is present – six wire wheels, dual sidemounts in canvas covers, twin spot lamps, dual trumpet horns and a big rear trunk.

1911 *bottom left* and 1913 four-cylinder Cadillacs. Both have right-hand steering but the older car, with its right-hand brake and gearshift levers, has only three doors to the 1913's four, hence the earlier car's side-mounted spare tire and rim: by 1913 these had moved to the back. Other changes are: electric rather than gas lights by 1913, a streamlined metal dash replacing a straight one in varnished wood, and nickel (not much of it, either) instead of brass brightwork. Both cars have the same type of four-cylinder motor, but the 1913 unit is a lot bigger, at 336 ci. On the later model's right-hand runningboard can be seen an electric klaxon (standard) and a telescopic trunk rack (extra).

The Series-370 Twelve was almost as impressive as the Sixteen – four fewer cylinders, a wheelbase eight inches shorter, and 30 fewer advertised horsepower. This one is the Fleetwood All-Weather Phaeton costing $4,895, complete with wire wheels, and sidemounts with covers and mirrors. The enamelled badge *center* on the radiator stoneguard spelt out the number of cylinders in that neat, plainly-finished, 45-degree valve-in-head motor *right*. The fascia *top left* is innocent of latter-day Detroit stylistic influences.

Series 345 LaSalle Fleetwood roadster, 1930. Maybe it's too close to a Cadillac with 340 ci of V-8 under the hood against the senior make's 355, an output only slightly inferior, and a wheelbase six inches shorter. The beauty is unquestionable, but the sort of folk who appreciated LaSalle's better acceleration and gas mileage bought secondhand, not new. Just visible are the cowl louvers which distinguished Fleetwood coachwork from the cheaper Fishers.

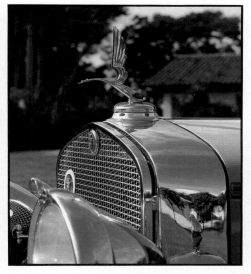

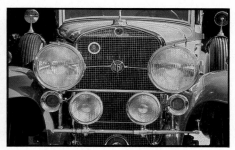

V-16 customers got twin spot lamps where eights and twelves usually made do with one. One almost never saw Cadillacs of this era without a stone-guard, either. The heron mascot *left* was a factory option from 1929 to 1933, the alternative being the first of the Cadillac goddesses.

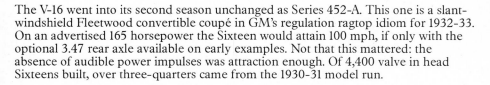

The V-16 went into its second season unchanged as Series 452-A. This one is a slant-windshield Fleetwood convertible coupé in GM's regulation ragtop idiom for 1932-33. On an advertised 165 horsepower the Sixteen would attain 100 mph, if only with the optional 3.47 rear axle available on early examples. Not that this mattered: the absence of audible power impulses was attraction enough. Of 4,400 valve in head Sixteens built, over three-quarters came from the 1930-31 model run.

V-16 roadsters – a 1930 452 by Fisher *left* and a 1931 452-A by Fleetwood *above*. Both wear Goddess mascots, but the twin spots have been omitted from the Fisher car, which also features the standard (but rare) wood wheels and demountable rims. 1930's Cadillac V-8s also had hood louvers, not doors, though these latter were adopted across the range in 1931. V-16 prices started at $5,395 in 1930, but at only $4,495 in 1931.

$2,945 worth of 1931 eight-cylinder dual-cowl phaeton, complete with all the usual extras: twin spot lamps, and a Goddess mascot, plus the hood louvers first seen on 1930's Sixteens. Whitewall tires, curiously, were seldom worn when this car was new, being usually the prerogative of formal town carriages.

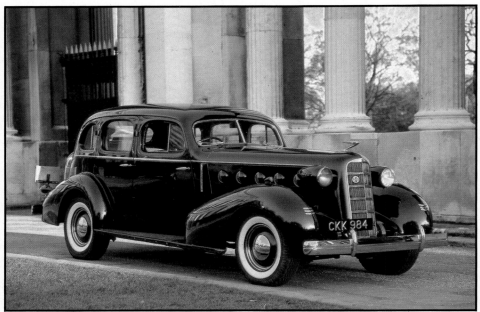

Right: the style-leading Cadillac Sixty Special in 1939 guise, with its thin pillars, vestigial running-boards, and the European 'sports saloon' look. The second season's three piece grille improved the appearance: the heavy sidemounts (compulsory on the British market) do not. The late '38 Oxford City license plate makes one wonder if this Cadillac started life as an example for study by Morris' engineers. They'd have found a lot to learn, especially in the suspension department.

Four lesser lights from the Cadillac galaxy. The 1935 LaSalle Series-50 *top left* was the Division's only eight-in-line and had affinities with the Oldsmobile, though Jules Agramonte's styling was exclusive. Altogether heavier is the 1938 seven-passenger Cadillac 75 *top right* with that season's aggressive grille; the red duco gives it less dignity than the earlier 1936 version *right* with very similar engineering. Sleek and individual is the penultimate LaSalle *above*, a 1939 convertible and a V-8 once more.

The American Custom Body Era was over by 1940. Shown *this page* is one of only three long-chassis Model-75 V-8s of the 1940 model run supplied to custom coachbuilders, in this case Brunn of Buffalo, usually associated with Lincolns. The cowl is stock Cadillac, but the rest is Custom, not the more familiar padded-top modification of a limousine. Price is not on record, but this one would have cost a lot more than the $3,360 asked for the regular seven-passenger Imperial. It is hard to see what a specialist coachbuilder could have done with the 1947 Model-62 convertible *facing page*, still a flathead V-8 of 346 ci, and still with a separate chassis riding on semi-elliptics at the rear. The shape is warmed-over 1942, with only minor changes, but automatic transmissions were on the march, and very few '47s would have come factory-equipped with anything other than four-speed Hydramatic.

This 1950 Coupé de Ville with valve-in-head motor *bottom left and right* is one of two Cadillacs raced that year at Le Mans by Briggs Cunningham; it placed tenth at an average speed of 81.54 mph. The vast 1947 Model-75 on the 136-inch wheelbase *below* has the older L-head engine and has been modified by Derham into a formal sedan by the deletion of the rear quarter-windows and the addition of landau irons and a fabric top.

Changing shapes. Running-boards and three-window styling survive on the 1941 Model-67 sedan *facing page*, on the long, 138-inch wheelbase, its Fisher-built body given the Fleetwood interior treatment. It's also one of the first Cadillacs with Hydramatic, regular equipment on the 1950 Model-62 sedan *below*, one of the cheapest (at $3,234) and certainly the best-selling (41,890 units) of the season's offerings. The dummy rear-fender air intake is in fashion, too.

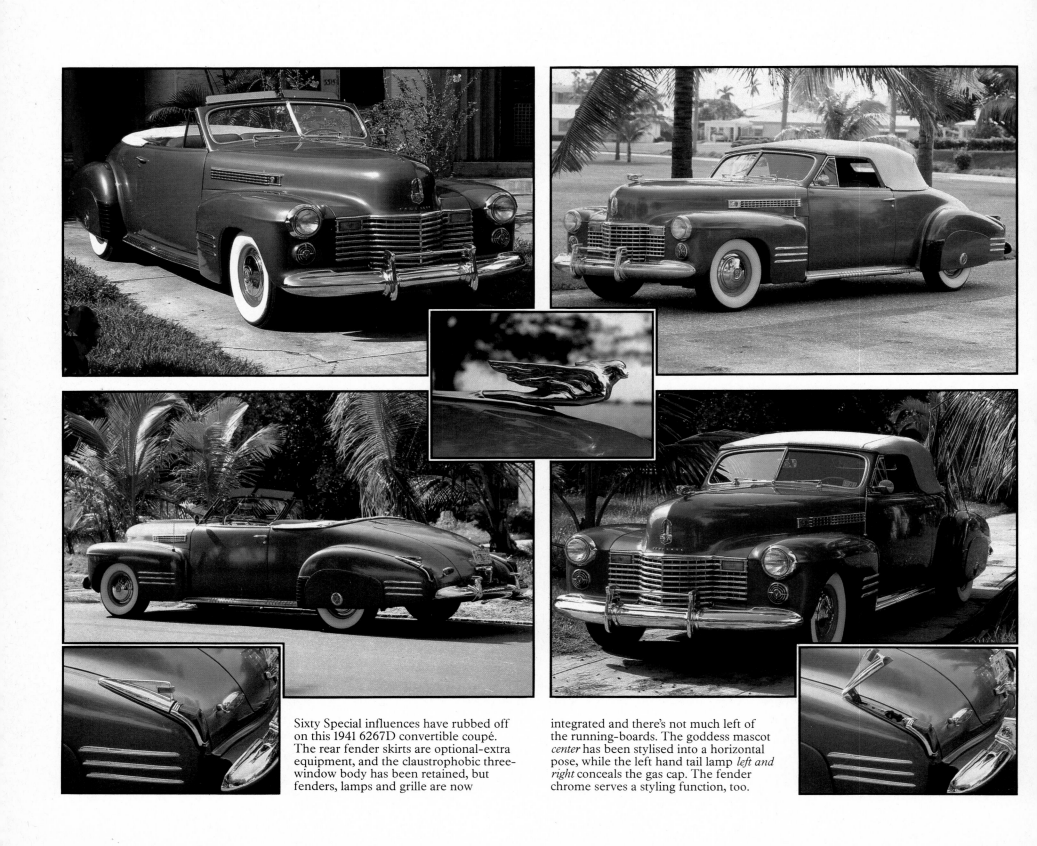

Sixty Special influences have rubbed off on this 1941 6267D convertible coupé. The rear fender skirts are optional-extra equipment, and the claustrophobic three-window body has been retained, but fenders, lamps and grille are now integrated and there's not much left of the running-boards. The goddess mascot *center* has been stylised into a horizontal pose, while the left hand tail lamp *left and right* conceals the gas cap. The fender chrome serves a styling function, too.

Back to the 1940 Brunn Town Car *facing page* and the 1947 Model-62 convertible. For all its stylised treatment, 1947's grille is simpler and easier to keep clean. And one can't really compare a ragtop (built to drive) with a formal (to be driven in). Under the hood, the later flathead *below* is somewhat cluttered up by its air cleaner and other ancillaries. The Model-62 really looks its best from the rear *bottom left*, with a top that tucks away neatly out of sight and an unadorned tail treatment without the 1938's P-38-inspired fins.

A World War separates these two vehicles, the 1941 Sixty Special and the 1948 62 on the *facing page*. On the mechanical side, differences are less than dramatic: as can be seen in the interior shots *far right* of the earlier car, it has already acquired an automatic transmission with the characteristic column-mounted selector and extended brake pedal, made possible by the absence of a clutch. The L-head motor is still with us, in essence a 1936 redesign of a theme going back to 1915. The stylist, however, waits for no man and yearly changes have not really improved the Sixty Special in its fourth season. The chromium-encrusted radiator grille has made a successful takeover bid for the fenders and has overflowed into them, and an extended fender line has eliminated the sidemount. Rear fender skirts are optional, but the ugly hood louvers are compulsory. The Cadillac crest *center* sits proudly on he trunk lid. On the new-look '48, integration has been completed, with the total style-in of bumpers and parking lights, and a curved windshield. Slab sides need side chromium for aesthetic as well as protective reasons, while the famed tail fins make their first, rather tentative appearance.

The 1955 Model-62 convertible is an enormous car, 216 inches long and 80 inches wide. The grille is still unmistakably Cadillac, however, and the ponderous dummy air intakes of the early 50s have faded into a minor outburst in vertical chromium. Typical of the period is the full wrap-round 'dog's leg' windshield, introduced to Cadillac the previous year. The latest 331 ci V-8 pushed out 250 horsepower on a 9:1 compression.

At the top of the post-World War II range was the Fleetwood 75, or luxury for nine. And if a regular Cadillac seemed big, this one's vital statistics were formidable: a wheelbase just short of 150 inches, a bumper to bumper length of 236 inches and a dry weight well over 5,000 pounds. Four cigar lighters, two electric clocks, and power brakes, seats, windows and divider were part of this 1956 package; air conditioning was an established regular option. Paintwork was usually black, although interior fabrics came in a pretty wide choice of broadcloths or Bedford Cords. Demand was limited but steady at 1,500-2,000 units a year during the 50s. The 75 wasn't, of course, the largest Cadillac: one step further still was the Professional Car Chassis for ambulance and hearse bodies which ran to 158 inches of wheelbase in 1956.

1957's super-car; the Eldorado Brougham with air suspension, cost $13,074, as against $6,648 for the exotic Eldorado Biarritz convertible, and a mere $4,713 for a 62 sedan. Styling was four-door pillarless hardtop *below* and the brushed stainless steel top shows up well in these pictures. Detail was most elaborate, as witness the smoker's companion *top right* and the big glovebox on the facia *top left* which came complete with six magnetised tumblers, cigarette case, lipstick, and stick cologne.

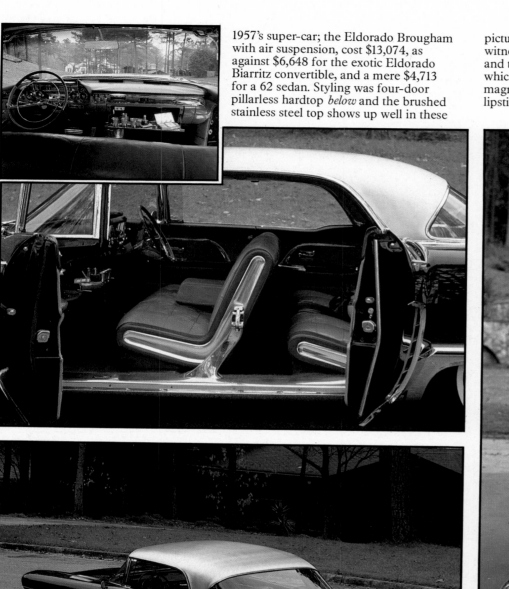

Again the 1957 Eldorado Brougham, its aggressive front end treatment and tusk-like bumpers much in evidence, though its stance at rest, was never as unhappy-looking as the Citroën D's. Other noteworthy features are forged wheels with their aluminum centers (rims were steel) and the ever-present tail fins. It looks big and it is – over 216 inches long and 78½ inches wide.

With the windows up, the 1957 Eldorado Brougham presents a conventional sedan appearance belied by the doors-open interior view *right* showing one of the 45 catalogued trim options. Two cigar lighters, all-transistor AM radio with automatic antenna, and tinted glass were standard, too.

Fin and tail-light treatment *left*. Other equipment included automatic door locks, electrically-operated trunk lid, quadruple horns, and a six-way power front seat with built-in memory. The air bag suspension, alas, had its problems, and Cadillac lost money on each one of the 704 Broughams they built.

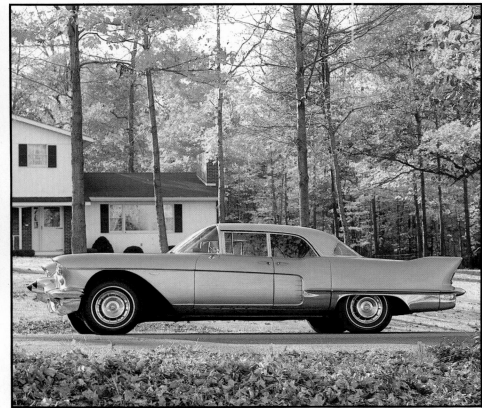

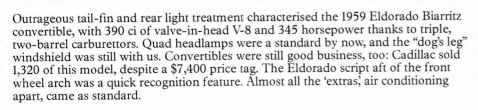

Outrageous tail-fin and rear light treatment characterised the 1959 Eldorado Biarritz convertible, with 390 ci of valve-in-head V-8 and 345 horsepower thanks to triple, two-barrel carburettors. Quad headlamps were a standard by now, and the "dog's leg" windshield was still with us. Convertibles were still good business, too: Cadillac sold 1,320 of this model, despite a $7,400 price tag. The Eldorado script aft of the front wheel arch was a quick recognition feature. Almost all the 'extras', air conditioning apart, came as standard.

Gasoline was still cheap, congestion problems as yet unfaced, and seat belts confined to the catalog's small print when this 1959 Cadillac 62 convertible was built, one of an impressive 11,130 to leave the factory that year. Total model-year production was 142,272 units. With only a single quadrajet carburettor on this version of the 390 ci motor, output was down to 320 horsepower. A full length side rubbing strip is the easiest way to tell the cheaper ragtop from the Biarritz.

Two more 1959 Cadillacs from the base 62 range – the Coupé de Ville *this page* and the Sedan de Ville *facing page*. The cars featured a 130-inch wheelbase and the 325-horsepower version of the V-8 motor, while power assistance for pretty well everything was optional, but not included in the list prices – $5,252 for the two-door and $5,498 for the four-door. Rear fender skirts were standard, the tail fins were matched by an equally aggressive grille, and there was also a mini-grille at the rear *top left*.

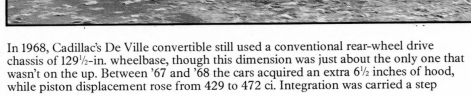

In 1968, Cadillac's De Ville convertible still used a conventional rear-wheel drive chassis of 129½-in. wheelbase, though this dimension was just about the only one that wasn't on the up. Between '67 and '68 the cars acquired an extra 6½ inches of hood, while piston displacement rose from 429 to 472 ci. Integration was carried a step further by parking the windshield wipers out of sight, where they sometimes stayed, thanks to snow and fall leaves. Convertible production stayed steady at around 18,000 units a year.

Front wheel drive or; what Oldsmobile thought last year Cadillac thinks today. Their first (1967) new generation Eldorado Fleetwood hardtop came a year behind the Olds Toronado, and was built on similar principles. Oldsmobile, however, didn't include such refinements as variable ratio power steering and automatic level control, and though the new Cadillac shared its body with the Olds and Buick's Riviera, it was still every inch a Cadillac. An impressive hood meant more than compact dimensions, so a short wheelbase did not make for a much smaller car. The 'formal' roofline presaged the hardtops of the '70s. Power front disc brakes were standard from the start.

1971's second-generation Eldorado, destined to be the basis for all Cadillac's remaining convertibles. It's some 222 inches long – front-wheel drive is no space-saver when combined with a north-south engine. This *center* is a hefty piece of machinery displacing 500 ci or 8.2 liters, even if a lower compression ratio gives 365 horsepower that would have sounded sedate a few years back. A massive look is imparted by the energy absorbing bumpers and the coffin-nose hood *right*.

1966 saw the last of the Eldorado convertibles and the last of the giant engines, since Cadillac went down to 425 ci in 1977. This car had four-wheel disc brakes and was available with electronic fuel injection. Shown is one of 200 'limited edition' white cars which marked (or so they thought) the end of the ragtop era. Cadillac had, however, already delivered another 13,800 standard cars before this publicity gesture. List price was $11,049, but in that summer's brief auction boom new examples were changing hands for over twenty grand.

Twilight of the giants: the 1977 Fleetwood Eldorado *below, bottom and facing page* was still a very big car, 224 in long and turning the scales at 4,955 pounds. Like all that season's full size Cadillacs, it used the 425 ci V-8, but it was now offered only as a pillared hardtop coupé, an extension of the original 1967 stylistic theme, but with the latest coffin-nose hood. Surprisingly, the 425 would continue into 1979, though by this time there'd be a diesel Eldorado as well.

A mid-1975 introduction, the Seville *above and top* marked a return to compact proportions and a hint of the European idiom not seen since the days of the original Sixty Special. Its overall dimensions – a wheelbase of 114 in. and a length of 204 in. – were modest, while fuel injection was standard. By 1979, when this car was built, all-disc brakes were standard, too, and you could have your Seville with gasoline or diesel V-8 motors, the latter made by Oldsmobile.

Light can have curious effects – all these pictures show the same car, a 1980 Cadillac Seville Elegante sedan in two-tone metallic silver. It features front wheel drive and all-disc brakes, with a choice of either a 368 ci gasoline or 350 ci diesel V-8 motor.

Engineering rationalisation at General Motors threatened to jeopardize Cadillac's individuality. The bustle-back, razor-edge sedan body was, however, peculiar to Seville. It is curiously reminiscent of Hooper's early post-War Rolls Royce.

1981 Eldorado Biarritz coupé, now on the Seville's short, 114-inch, wheelbase and weighing under 4,000 pounds. The big news here was Cadillac's 'modulated displacement' motor *center*, automatically set up to run on four, six or eight cylinders according to road conditions. It was still a large engine (368 ci) but it is perhaps significant that in 1982 its use was restricted to the big 75 limousine.

Also fitted for 1981 with the 368 ci modulated-displacement engine was the full-size Fleetwood Brougham, now almost with a big-Mercedes look about it, and styling derived from the original 1975 Seville. On big Cadillacs, rear drive and ladder-type frames were retained: the engine option list included not only the usual V-8 diesel but the Division's first-ever six, of 252 cu. in. It was a 90-degree vee built by Buick.

'Cimarron by Cadillac': never referred to in press releases as the Cadillac Cimarron. From the Cadillac standpoint it combined just about every heresy in the book, being a small car with four-cylinder transverse motor *center* driving the front wheels, and close affinities with parallel Chevrolets. It was also the Division's first four since the demise of the Thirty in 1914, and the first Cadillac in nearly thirty years with manual transmission, though the interior shot *top left* shows the optional 'stick automatic'. At least the grille was Cadillac.

1983 Cimarron: the shape is little changed, but the latest fuel injected four-cylinder motor has been enlarged to 122 ci, the manual transmission option has five forward speeds instead of four, and regular equipment now includes rectangular foglamps under the front bumper, and alloy wheels. But it's still another J-car, with close relatives carrying lesser badges at home and an assortment of foreign ones abroad.

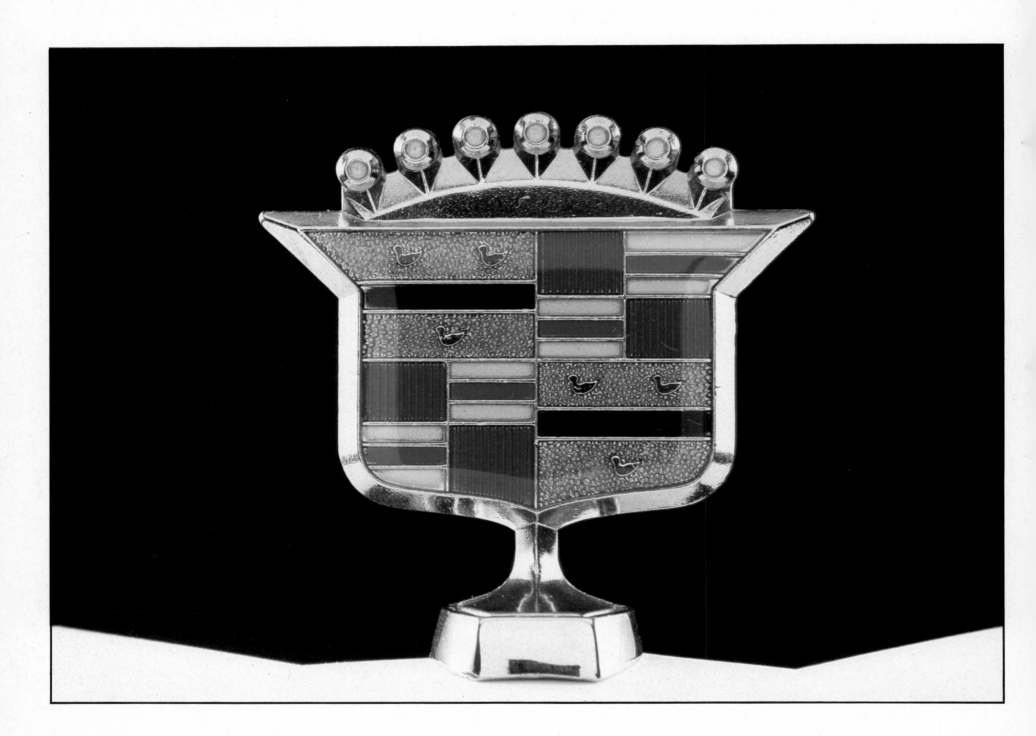